Words to Teenager

BRAHMACHARIMAYUM DEVDUTTA SHARMA

Title   :   Words to Teenager

Author   :   Brahmacharimayum Devdutta Sharma

Edition   :   First (July, 2024)

ISBN   :   9788197599613

Published by

| TANEESHA PUBLISHERS | A Venture by - PRACHI DIGITAL PUBLICATION |

Regd. Add.: 254, Khuriyakhatta No. 10, Bindukhatta, Lalkuan, Nainital - 262402, Uttarakhand, India
Website : www.taneeshapublishers.in
E-mail : taneeshapublishers@gmail.com
Phone : +91 845481 2712, +91 976041 7980

Printed by :
Manipal Technologies Limited, Bengaluru - 560001, Karnataka

INDEX

INDEX

About the Book

The world we live in today is rapidly evolving. Technology has taken over almost every aspect of our lives, from how we communicate to how we work and even how we learn. This digitalization era has brought about immense changes and advancements, making our lives easier and more convenient. However, as teenagers, are we truly aware of the impact this digitalization has on us?

The digitalization era has its pros and cons, and it is up to us, as teenagers, to use technology wisely. It can be a blessing if we use it as a tool while being mindful of its negative effects. However, it can become a curse if we let it consume our lives and dictate our actions. So let us use technology as a tool for growth and development rather than becoming slaves to it.

Remember, we are the generation that will shape the future, so let us use technology responsibly and make the most out of this digitalization era.

"Words to Teenagers" is a thought-provoking book that delves into the impact of digitalization on the younger generation. This book offers valuable insights and practical advice for teenagers navigating the digital world. The authors emphasize the importance of using technology in a balanced and responsible manner, highlighting the potential risks of excessive screen time, social media usage, and online interactions.

They provide tips on how teenagers can cultivate healthy digital habits, protect their privacy online, and stay safe in the digital realm. With engaging real-life examples and relatable anecdotes, "Words to Teenagers" encourages readers to think critically about their digital footprint, online relationships, and mental well-being in the age of smartphones and social media. The book also addresses topics such as cyberbullying, digital literacy, and the future of work in a digitalized world.

Overall, this book serves as a timely and informative guide for teenagers seeking guidance on how to navigate the complexities of digitalization responsibly and confidently.

Chapter ~ 1

The Dawn of Digitalization : Embracing the Future

The world is rapidly evolving and technology is at the forefront of this transformation. From smartphones to smart homes, digitalization has become an integral part of our lives. The rise of digitalization has brought about significant changes in the way we live, work, and communicate. It has completely reshaped industries, revolutionized business models, and transformed the global economy. But what exactly is digitalization?

Simply put, it is the process of using technology to convert analog information into digital formats. In simpler terms, it is the shift from traditional methods to digital technologies.

With the increasing use of computers, internet, and mobile devices, digitalization has become a way of life.

The concept of digitalization may seem like a recent phenomenon, but its roots can be traced back to the mid-20th century when computers were first introduced. However, it was not until the late 20th century that digitalization truly took off with the advent of personal computers and the internet.

The dawn of digitalization has brought about numerous benefits and opportunities for individuals and businesses alike. Let's take a closer look at how it has impacted our world.

1. Efficiency and Productivity:

One of the major advantages of digitalization is its ability to streamline processes and increase efficiency. With the use of digital tools and platforms, tasks that once took hours can now be completed in a matter of minutes. This has resulted in higher productivity levels and faster turnaround times for businesses.

For individuals, digitalization has made daily tasks such as banking, shopping, and communication much more convenient and efficient. With just a few clicks, we can now transfer funds, purchase goods, and connect with people from all over the world.

2. Global Connectivity

Digitalization has also brought people closer together by breaking down geographical barriers. With internet access and social media platforms, we can now connect with individuals from different parts of the world and share ideas and information instantly. This has opened up numerous opportunities for collaboration, learning, and growth. Businesses have also benefited from this global connectivity and can now reach a wider audience through digital marketing and e-commerce. Small businesses, in particular, have been able to expand their customer base and compete on a global scale due to digitalization.

3. Automation and Innovation

Digitalization has paved the way for automation, which has revolutionized industries such as manufacturing, transportation, and healthcare. With the use of robots and artificial intelligence, tasks that were once done manually can now be performed with greater accuracy and efficiency.

Moreover, digitalization has sparked a culture of innovation, with new technologies being developed every day to make our lives easier. From voice assistants to self-driving cars, these innovations are constantly pushing the boundaries of what is possible.

4. Data and Analytics

With digitalization, businesses now have access to vast amounts of data that can be analyzed to gain insights into consumer behavior, market trends, and business performance. This allows them to make data-driven decisions and tailor their products and services according to the needs of their customers.

For individuals, digitalization has also

made it easier to track their health and fitness goals through wearable devices and mobile applications. This data can then be used to make informed decisions about one's well-being.

5. Flexibility and Mobility

Digitalization has also brought about a shift in the way we work. With remote working becoming more common, individuals now have the flexibility to work from anywhere as long as they have an internet connection. This has not only improved work-life balance but also reduced commute time and costs.

Moreover, mobile devices have made it possible for us to carry out tasks on the go. Whether it's checking emails, attending virtual meetings or accessing important documents, we can now stay connected and productive even when we are away from our desks.

With all these benefits in mind, it is clear that digitalization has changed the world in more ways than one. However, like any other major change, it also comes with its own set of challenges.

One of the main concerns surrounding digitalization is the threat it poses to job security. As technology continues to advance, some jobs are becoming obsolete while new ones are being created. This has led to a growing demand for individuals with digital skills and has highlighted the need for continuous learning and upskilling.

Moreover, digitalization has also raised issues regarding data privacy and security. With the vast amount of personal information being stored and shared online, there is a constant risk of data breaches and cyber attacks. It is crucial for individuals and businesses to take necessary measures to protect their data.

So what does the future hold for digitalization? It's safe to say that it will continue to shape our world in ways we cannot even imagine. With the rise of technologies such as artificial intelligence, blockchain, and 5G, we can expect even more advancements and changes in the years to come.

As we embrace the dawn of digitalization, it is important to remember that it is not about replacing traditional methods but rather finding ways to integrate them with new technologies. It is about finding a balance between human interaction and technological advancements.

In conclusion, digitalization has significantly transformed our world and will continue to do so in the future. It has brought numerous benefits and opportunities, but it also comes with its own set of challenges. As we move forward into a more digitalized world, it is important to adapt and embrace this change while also being mindful of its impact on society.

Chapter - 2

Embracing Technology as Teenagers

Technology has become an inseparable part of our lives, and as teenagers, we have grown up in a world where it is constantly evolving and becoming more advanced.

It is no surprise that we are often referred to as the "digital natives" or the "tech-savvy generation". We are the ones who have adapted quickly to the latest gadgets, apps, and social media platforms. But with all this access to technology, there comes a responsibility to use it wisely and in a way that benefits us.

The Benefits of Technology for Teenagers

Technology has opened up a world of

opportunities for us as teenagers. It has made learning more interactive and engaging with the use of educational apps and online resources. We can now access information on any topic with just a few clicks, which has made studying and research much easier.

Moreover, technology has also made communication more convenient and efficient. We can stay connected with our friends and family through various messaging apps, video calls, and social media platforms. This has helped us maintain relationships even when we are physically apart.

Technology has also provided us with endless entertainment options. We can stream our favorite movies and TV shows, listen to music, and play video games on our devices. It has also given rise to new forms of entertainment like vlogging, creating content for social media platforms, and online streaming services.

Embracing technology has also given us a sense of independence and responsibility. With access to smartphones, we can navigate our way around the city, keep track of our schedules, and even manage our finances through mobile banking apps.

The Importance of Responsible Technology Use

While technology has its numerous benefits, it is essential for us as teenagers to use it responsibly. With all the information available at our fingertips, it is easy to get lost in the virtual world and lose touch with reality. We must remember that technology should enhance our lives, not consume it.

One of the most crucial aspects of responsible technology use is being aware of our screen time. With multiple devices and social media platforms, it is easy to spend hours scrolling through our feeds, watching videos, or playing games. However, excessive screen time can have negative effects on our mental and physical health. It is essential to take breaks and limit our screen time to maintain a healthy balance.

Another aspect of responsible technology use

is being mindful of our online presence. With the rise of social media, we are constantly sharing our thoughts, pictures, and personal information online. While this can be a great way to connect with others, it is essential to think before we post.

We must remember that anything we put out on the internet stays there forever, and it can have consequences in the future. It is crucial to respect our privacy and that of others while using social media.

Technology has also made it easier for us to access inappropriate content. As teenagers, we must be aware of the risks and dangers of accessing such content and refrain from doing so. We should also be cautious when interacting with strangers online and never share personal information with them.

Using Technology for Positive Impact

As teenagers, we have the power to use technology for positive change in society. We can use social media platforms to raise awareness about important issues, share our opinions and ideas, and support causes that are important to us. We have seen numerous examples of how teenagers have utilized technology to bring about change, whether it is through starting a social movement or raising funds for a charitable cause.

Moreover, technology has also opened up opportunities for us to learn new skills and pursue our passions. We can enroll in online courses, participate in webinars and workshops, and even start our own online businesses. The possibilities are endless when we embrace technology with a positive mindset.

In conclusion, as teenagers, we must embrace technology but with responsibility and mindfulness. We should use it to enhance our lives, stay connected with others, and make a positive impact on society. Let us use our "digital native" status to our advantage and pave the way for a better future.

Chapter - 3

Navigating the Virtual World Safely : Tips and Tricks for Staying Protected Online

In today's digital age, technology has become an integral part of our daily lives. From social media to online shopping, we are constantly connected to the virtual world. While this has made our lives more convenient, it has also opened up a whole new realm of potential threats and dangers. Cybercrime and online fraud are on the rise, making it crucial for us to learn how to navigate the virtual world safely. In this blog, we will discuss some tips and tricks to help you stay protected online.

1. Create Strong and Unique Passwords One of the simplest yet most effective

ways to protect yourself online is by creating strong and unique passwords for all your online accounts. Avoid using common passwords like "123456" or "password" as they are easy for hackers to guess. Instead, use a combination of uppercase and lowercase letters, numbers, and special characters or local language to create a strong password. Also, make sure to use different passwords for different accounts, as using the same password for multiple accounts can put all your information at risk if one account gets hacked.

2. Be Careful with Personal Information

In the virtual world, we often share personal information without much thought. However, this information can be used by cybercriminals to steal our identity or commit fraud. Therefore, it is important to be cautious about what personal information we share online.

Avoid sharing sensitive information like your

address, phone number, date of birth, or social security number on social media or other public platforms. Also, be wary of emails or messages asking for personal information, as they could be phishing attempts.

3. Keep Your Software and Devices Updated

Updating your software and devices may seem like a tedious task, but it is crucial for staying protected online. Software updates often include security patches that fix vulnerabilities in the system and protect you from cyber threats. Similarly, keeping your devices updated ensures that they have the latest security features.

Set your devices to automatically update, so you don't have to worry about manually checking for updates.

4. Use Two-Factor Authentication

Two-factor authentication (2FA) is an additional layer of security that requires you to enter a code or use a physical device, such as a fingerprint or facial recognition, along with your password to access your accounts. This makes it harder for hackers to gain access to your accounts, as they would need both your password and the physical device or code. Many online platforms offer 2FA as an option, and it is highly recommended to enable it for added security.

5. Be Cautious of Public Wi-Fi

We often use public Wi-Fi at cafes, airports, or hotels without much thought. However, public Wi-Fi networks are not secure and can leave your personal information vulnerable to hackers. Avoid logging into sensitive accounts or making online purchases while connected to public Wi-Fi. If you must use public Wi-Fi, consider using a virtual private network (VPN) to encrypt your data and protect your online activities.

6. Educate Yourself About Scams

Scammers are constantly coming up with new ways to trick people into giving away their personal information or money. It is essential to educate yourself about common online scams and how to identify them. Some common scams include phishing emails, fake websites, and fraudulent phone calls. Be wary of any unsolicited messages or requests for personal information, and always double-check the authenticity of a website before entering any sensitive information.

7. Limit Your Social Media Exposure

Social media has become a significant part of our lives, but it also exposes us to potential risks and threats. Hackers can use the information we share on social media platforms to gather personal information and commit identity theft or fraud. Therefore, it is important to limit the amount of personal information you share on social media and to review your privacy settings regularly. You can also consider using a pseudonym or a nickname instead of your real name on social media.

8. Use Reliable Security Software

Investing in reliable security software, such as antivirus and anti-malware programs, is crucial for staying protected online. These programs can detect and prevent malicious software from infecting your devices and stealing your information. Make sure to keep these programs updated and run regular scans to ensure your devices are protected.

9. Monitor Your Bank and Credit Card Statements

In the virtual world, it is easier for hackers to steal your financial information and make unauthorized transactions without you even realizing it. Therefore, it is important to regularly monitor your bank and credit card statements for any suspicious or unauthorized transactions. If you notice any, report it to your bank immediately to prevent further fraud.

10. Trust Your Instincts

Lastly, always trust your instincts when navigating the virtual world. If something seems too good to be true or feels off, it's best to err on the side of caution. Don't click on suspicious links or open emails from unknown senders, and never give out your personal information unless you are confident about the source.

In conclusion, the virtual world offers us endless opportunities and convenience, but it also comes with its fair share of risks. By following these tips and tricks, you can navigate the virtual world safely and protect yourself from cyber threats and fraud. Remember, staying safe online is a continuous effort, so make sure to stay updated with the latest security measures and trust your instincts when needed.

Chapter - 4

Social Media Etiquette : The Dos and Don'ts

In today's digital age, social media has become an integral part of our daily lives. From sharing photos and videos to connecting with friends and family, social media platforms have made it easier for us to stay connected and informed. However, with the increasing use of social media, it's important to be mindful of our actions and behavior online.

In this chapter, we will discuss the dos and don'ts of social media etiquette to help you navigate the digital world with grace and respect.

Dos:

1. Use proper language and tone

One of the key elements of social media etiquette is using proper language and tone. It's easy to get carried away with emotions and express ourselves in a negative or aggressive manner online. However, it's important to remember that our words have a lasting impact and can be seen by a wide audience. Therefore, always use respectful language and maintain a polite tone in your posts and comments.

2. Think before you post

We've all heard the phrase "think before you speak", but it's equally important to think before you post on social media. Once something is posted online, it's out there for the world to see, and it's not always easy to take it back. Before hitting that 'share' or 'post' button, ask yourself if the content aligns with your values and if it could potentially harm someone else. If in doubt, it's best to refrain from posting.

3. Give credit where credit is due

With the abundance of information available on the internet, it can be tempting to share content without giving credit to the original source. However, it's important to acknowledge and give credit to the creator of the content you share. This not only shows respect for their work but also avoids any potential copyright issues.

4. Engage in meaningful conversations

Social media is not just about posting content, but also about engaging in conversations with others. Be open to diverse opinions and engage in respectful discussions. Avoid getting into arguments or heated debates, and if you come across any offensive or inappropriate comments, it's best to ignore or report them.

5. Use privacy settings

Privacy is a major concern on social media, and it's important to take necessary measures to protect your personal information. Make use of privacy settings to control who can see your posts and personal information. It's also a good idea to review these settings regularly and make necessary adjustments.

Don'ts:

1. Overshare personal information

While social media is a great way to share updates with friends and family, it's important to be cautious about how much personal information you share. Avoid posting your full address, phone number, or any other sensitive information that could potentially compromise your safety.

2. Engage in cyberbullying

Cyberbullying has become a major issue on social media platforms, and it's important to not engage in such behavior. Avoid posting hurtful or negative comments towards others, and if you come across any form of cyberbullying, report it immediately.

3. Post inappropriate content

It's easy to get carried away with posting content that may seem funny or entertaining at the moment, but could potentially be offensive to others. Avoid posting content that could be seen as vulgar, discriminatory, or offensive towards any group of people.

4. Spamming

Constantly bombarding your followers with promotional posts or messages can be seen as spamming and can lead to people unfollowing you or even reporting you. Avoid excessive self-promotion and focus on creating meaningful and engaging content for your followers.

5. Neglecting online relationships

With the convenience of social media, it's easy to neglect our real-life relationships and solely rely on online interactions. It's important to maintain a balance between our online and offline interactions and not let social media consume all of our time and attention.

In conclusion, social media has become a powerful tool for communication and connection, but it's important to use it responsibly. By following these dos and don'ts of social media etiquette, we can create a positive and respectful online community. Remember to always think before you post and treat others with kindness and respect.

Chapter - 5

Finding a Balance: The Importance of Balancing Screen Time and Real Life

In today's digital age, it's no secret that screens dominate our lives. From smartphones and laptops to televisions and gaming consoles, screens have become an integral part of our daily routines. While technology has undoubtedly brought numerous benefits and conveniences, it has also resulted in many individuals becoming reliant on screens for various aspects of their lives.

As a result, finding a balance between screen time and real life has become increasingly challenging. We often find ourselves mindlessly scrolling through social media or binge-watching our favorite shows, neglecting our physical and mental well-being. It's essential to recognize the need for a balance between screen time and real life and understand its impact on our overall health and relationships.

The Effects of Excessive Screen Time While technology has undoubtedly made our lives more convenient, it also has its drawbacks. Spending too much time in front of screens can have adverse effects on our physical, mental, and emotional well-being.

One of the most significant impacts of excessive screen time is on our physical health. Sitting in front of a screen for extended periods can lead to a sedentary lifestyle, causing various health problems such as obesity, back and neck pain, and eye strain. Additionally, excessive screen time can disrupt our sleep patterns, leading to fatigue and reduced productivity.

Mentally, too much screen time can take a toll on our cognitive abilities. Constantly being connected to screens can overstimulate our brains, making it difficult to focus and concentrate. It can also lead to increased anxiety and stress levels as we become consumed by the constant stream of information and social comparisons.

Furthermore, excessive screen time can also have a significant impact on our relationships. Spending too much time on screens can result in neglecting face-to-face interactions with loved ones, leading to feelings of loneliness and disconnection. It can also cause conflicts in personal relationships as we become distracted and unavailable while engulfed in our digital world. Finding a Balance So, how can we find a balance between screen time and real life? The key is to be mindful of our screen usage and make conscious decisions to limit it. Here are some ways to achieve that:

1. **Set boundaries and limits:** Designate specific times of the day for screen usage and stick to it. For example, set a time limit for using social media or watching TV, and once the time is up, put away the screens and engage in other activities.

2. Prioritize real-life interactions: Instead of constantly texting or messaging loved ones, make an effort to spend quality time with them in person. Plan activities that don't involve screens, such as going for a walk or having a game night.

3. Engage in hobbies and activities: Find activities that you enjoy outside of screens, such as reading, painting, or exercising. These hobbies can help reduce screen time and also have numerous benefits for your overall well-being.

4. Disconnect regularly: Take breaks from screens throughout the day. Use this time to focus on yourself, relax, and recharge without any distractions.

5. Make your bedroom a screen-free zone: Avoid bringing screens into your bedroom as it can disrupt your sleep patterns. Instead, use this space for rest and relaxation.

The Importance of Balance

Finding a balance between screen time and real life is crucial for our overall well-being. It allows us to disconnect from the digital world and focus on ourselves and our relationships. Here are some benefits of finding this balance:

1. Improved physical health: Limiting screen time can help reduce the negative effects on our physical health, such as obesity and eye strain. It also encourages us to engage in physical activities, leading to a healthier lifestyle.

2. Better mental health: Disconnecting from screens can help reduce stress levels, improve focus, and increase mindfulness. It also allows us to be present in the moment and appreciate our surroundings.

3. Stronger relationships: By limiting screen time, we can prioritize spending quality time with loved ones, leading to stronger relationships and deeper connections.

4. Increased productivity: When we spend less time mindlessly scrolling through screens, we have more time to focus on our tasks and be more productive.

5. Enhanced creativity: Engaging in activities outside of screens can boost our creativity and imagination. It also provides a break from the constant stream of information and allows our minds to recharge.

In conclusion, finding a balance between screen time and real life is crucial for our physical, mental, and emotional well-being. It allows us to disconnect from the digital world and focus on what truly matters - our relationships, physical health, and personal growth. So let's make a conscious effort to limit our screen time and find a healthy balance that works for us.

Chapter - 6

The Power of Digital Literacy

In today's fast-paced and technology-driven world, being digitally literate is essential for personal and professional success. Digital literacy refers to the ability to navigate, evaluate, and communicate information effectively through various digital mediums such as computers, smartphones, and the internet. With the rapid growth of technology and its integration into our daily lives, it has become crucial to possess digital literacy skills to thrive in this digital age.

The power of digital literacy lies in its ability to bridge the gap between individuals and the ever-evolving digital world. It enables people to access a vast amount of information, communicate with others, and create and share content with just a few clicks. With the advancement of technology, the ways in which we consume and interact with information have drastically changed. Digital literacy allows individuals to adapt to these changes and stay informed in a constantly evolving digital landscape.

One of the significant advantages of digital literacy is its impact on education. With the rise of e-learning platforms, online courses, and virtual classrooms, students now have access to a wealth of knowledge at their fingertips. Digital literacy skills such as effective internet research, critical thinking, and online communication are essential for students to excel in their education. It also allows students to collaborate and participate in global discussions with individuals from different parts of the world, providing them with a diverse and enriching learning experience.

Furthermore, digital literacy has also revolutionized the way we work. With remote work becoming increasingly popular, having digital literacy skills is crucial for individuals to be productive and efficient in their jobs. The ability to use various digital tools and platforms allows employees to work remotely without any hindrance. It also provides them with the flexibility to balance work and personal life while staying connected with their colleagues and clients.

Digital literacy also plays a significant role in empowering individuals in their personal lives. With easy access to information on health, wellness, finance, and other areas, individuals can make informed decisions and take control of their lives. Social media platforms have also become a powerful tool for individuals to connect with others, share their thoughts and ideas, and build communities based on common interests. Digital literacy skills such as online communication, digital etiquette, and online safety are crucial in maintaining healthy and meaningful relationships in the digital world.

Moreover, digital literacy has also opened up numerous opportunities for entrepreneurship and creativity. The internet has made it easier for individuals to start their own businesses and reach a global audience. With digital marketing, social media advertising, and e-commerce platforms, entrepreneurs can reach potential customers worldwide without geographical limitations. Digital literacy skills such as content creation, digital marketing, and data analysis are essential for entrepreneurs to succeed in today's competitive market.

The power of digital literacy is not limited to individuals but also extends to society as a whole. With the rise of social media, individuals now have the ability to voice their opinions and bring attention to important issues. Digital literacy allows individuals to research and fact-check information, promoting critical thinking and responsible sharing of information. It also enables individuals to stay informed about current events and participate in discussions and debates that shape our society.

However, with its power comes the responsibility to use digital literacy ethically and responsibly. The internet has made it easier for misinformation and fake news to spread quickly, leading to significant consequences. Therefore, digital literacy also involves understanding the importance of online privacy, security, and ethical behavior. It is crucial for individuals to be aware of the potential risks and consequences of their actions in the digital world.

In conclusion, the power of digital literacy lies in its ability to connect us with the world and empower us to navigate through it effectively. It has transformed education, work, personal lives, entrepreneurship, and society as a whole. In today's world, being digitally literate is no longer an option but a necessity. As technology continues to advance at a rapid pace, it is essential for individuals to continuously update and enhance their digital literacy skills to stay informed and succeed in this digital age. So, let us embrace the power of digital literacy and use it to shape a better and more connected future for ourselves and the world.

Chapter- 7

The Importance of Online Etiquette and Cyberbullying Awareness in the Digital Age

In today's digital world, we are constantly connected to each other through social media, messaging apps, and other online platforms. While this has opened up a whole new world of opportunities and connectivity, it has also brought about some negative consequences such as cyberbullying.

As more and more people turn to the internet to communicate and socialize, it is crucial that we understand the importance of online etiquette and are aware of the impact of cyberbullying.

What is Online Etiquette?

Online etiquette, also known as netiquette, refers to the set of rules and guidelines that govern polite and respectful behavior in online interactions. Just like in face-to-face interactions, it is important to have good manners and follow certain etiquette in the virtual world as well. This includes being respectful towards others, using appropriate language and tone, avoiding offensive or discriminatory comments, and respecting people's privacy.

Why is Online Etiquette Important?

The internet is a vast and diverse space where people from different backgrounds come together to share their thoughts, opinions, and experiences. With so many people interacting with each other on a daily basis, it is important to have a code of conduct to ensure that everyone feels safe and respected. Good online etiquette helps create a positive online community where people can freely express themselves without fear of being attacked or bullied.

Moreover, practicing good online etiquette can also benefit an individual's personal and professional life. Many employers now conduct online background checks on potential employees, and having a good online presence with appropriate behavior can leave a positive impression. Additionally, maintaining good relationships with others online can lead to networking opportunities and open doors for potential collaborations.

The Dangers of Cyberbullying

Cyberbullying is defined as the use of electronic communication to bully, harass, or threaten someone. It can take various forms such as sending hurtful messages, sharing private information without consent, spreading rumors, or posting malicious comments on social media. The anonymity and perceived distance of the internet can make cyberbullying even more harmful, as the bully may not realize the impact of their actions on the victim.

The rise of social media and online platforms

has made cyberbullying an even bigger concern. According to a survey by the Cyberbullying Research Center, 36% of teenagers have experienced cyberbullying, and 17% have been cyberbullied in the past 30 days. The effects of cyberbullying can be devastating, leading to low self-esteem, anxiety, depression, and in some cases, even suicide.

The Role of Awareness in Preventing Cyberbullying

As with any issue, awareness is key in preventing and addressing cyberbullying. Parents, teachers, and other adults should educate themselves about the signs of cyberbullying and how to support victims. Children and teenagers should also be educated about the importance of online etiquette and the impact of their actions online.

It is also important for individuals to understand the consequences of cyberbullying, both legally and morally. Cyberbullying can have serious legal implications, as it is considered a form of harassment and can result in criminal charges.

Moreover, being a cyberbully can also have long-lasting effects on a person's reputation and relationships.

Tips for Practicing Good Online Etiquette

1. Think before you post: It is important to carefully consider the content and tone of your posts before hitting the "share" button. Ask yourself if your comment or post could be interpreted as offensive or hurtful to others.

2. Use respectful language: Just like in face-to-face interactions, using respectful language online is crucial for maintaining a positive community. Avoid using profanity or discriminatory language that may offend others.

3. Respect people's privacy: Always ask for permission before sharing someone else's photo or personal information. Respect their boundaries and remember that not everyone is comfortable with having their personal information shared online.

4. Be mindful of your tone: Tone can easily be misinterpreted online, as there are no nonverbal cues to convey emotions. Be mindful of the tone you use in your messages and try to avoid sarcasm or jokes that may be hurtful to others.

5. Don't engage in cyberbullying: If you come across any form of cyberbullying, do not engage with the bully. Report the incident to the appropriate authorities and offer support to the victim.

6. Be a positive influence: Use your online presence to spread positivity and kindness. Share uplifting messages, support others, and be a role model for good online behavior.

In conclusion, good online etiquette and cyberbullying awareness are crucial in today's digital age. By practicing good online etiquette, we can create a positive and respectful online community and prevent cyberbullying. It is important for individuals of all ages to educate themselves about these issues and actively work towards promoting a safe and inclusive online environment for everyone. Remember, our actions online can have real-life consequences, so let's strive to be kind and respectful in our online interactions.

Chapter -8

Harnessing Technology for Learning and Growth

In today's digital age, technology has become an integral part of our lives. From social media to online shopping, we use technology for almost everything. However, one of the most important areas where technology has made a significant impact is in the field of education. With the rapid advancements in technology, the traditional methods of learning and growth have been revolutionized, offering endless opportunities for students and professionals to enhance their skills and knowledge. In this blog, we will explore the various ways in which technology can be harnessed for learning and growth.

Access to Unlimited Information and Resources

One of the most significant advantages of technology in education is the access to unlimited information and resources. Gone are the days when students had to rely solely on textbooks and limited reference materials. With the internet at their fingertips, students can now access a vast array of information on any subject they desire. Online libraries, e-books, educational videos, and interactive learning tools are just a few examples of how technology has expanded the scope of learning. This not only makes the learning process more engaging but also allows students to explore different perspectives and broaden their knowledge.

Personalized Learning

Every student has a unique way of learning, and traditional classroom settings may not cater to individual needs. However, with technology, personalized learning has become a reality. Educational software and tools can analyze a student's strengths and weaknesses and provide personalized learning experiences tailored to their needs. This helps students learn at their own pace, making it easier for them to grasp complex concepts. Moreover, with the help of artificial intelligence (AI) and machine learning (ML), these tools can adapt and adjust according to a student's progress, ensuring maximum efficiency in learning.

Enhanced Collaboration and Communication

Technology has also transformed the way students collaborate and communicate with one another. With online platforms such as Google Docs and Microsoft Teams, students can work on group projects seamlessly, regardless of their physical location.

This not only promotes teamwork but also prepares students for the professional world, where virtual collaboration is becoming the norm. Additionally, with the popularity of video conferencing tools like Zoom and Skype, students can easily connect with their peers and teachers for discussions and learning sessions, making education more interactive and engaging.

Real-World Simulations and Virtual Reality

Another exciting aspect of technology in education is the use of real-world simulations and virtual reality (VR). These tools allow students to experience scenarios and environments that would otherwise be impossible in a traditional classroom setting.

For example, medical students can practice surgeries on virtual patients, while engineering students can simulate real-life construction projects. Such simulations not only enhance the learning experience but also provide practical knowledge that can be beneficial in a student's career.

Flexibility and Accessibility

Technology has made learning more flexible and accessible than ever before. Online learning platforms, such as Coursera and Udemy, offer a wide range of courses from top universities and industry professionals, making it possible for individuals to learn anytime and anywhere. This is especially beneficial for working professionals who may not have the time to attend regular classes. Additionally, technology has also made education more accessible to those with physical disabilities or geographical constraints, providing equal opportunities for learning and growth.

Continuous Learning

With the rise of e-learning and online courses, the concept of continuous learning has gained momentum. Technology has made it possible for individuals to learn new skills and acquire knowledge throughout their lives.

This is crucial in today's fast-paced world where new technologies and innovations are constantly emerging, requiring individuals to update their skills constantly. The accessibility of online courses also allows individuals to switch careers or pursue new interests without disrupting their current lifestyle.

Adaptability to Change

In today's rapidly evolving world, adaptability is a crucial skill for success. Technology plays a significant role in developing this skill through its constant advancements and updates. Students who are exposed to technology in their learning process are more likely to adapt to new technologies and changes in the future. This is essential for their future careers, where they will have to keep up with the latest trends and technological advancements.

In conclusion, technology has completely transformed the way we learn and grow. It has not only made education more accessible and flexible but has also enhanced the learning experience and prepared individuals for the future.

However, it is crucial to note that technology should be used as a tool to support and complement traditional methods of learning rather than replacing them entirely. With the right balance, we can harness technology's power for learning and growth, opening up endless possibilities for individuals to reach their full potential.

Chapter - 9

The Digital Age: Opening Doors to Limitless Career Opportunities

The digital age has brought about a massive transformation in the way we live, work, and interact with the world. With the rapid advancement of technology, the job market has also undergone a significant shift, opening doors to endless career opportunities for individuals across various industries. From traditional jobs to new, emerging roles, the digital age has created a plethora of options for individuals looking to kickstart their careers or make a change. Let's take a closer look at how the digital age has revolutionized the job market and what career opportunities it has brought along.

1. Remote Work

One of the most significant changes brought about by the digital age is the rise of remote work. With the help of technology, individuals can now work from anywhere in the world, breaking free from the constraints of a traditional office setup. This has opened up opportunities for individuals who may not have access to job opportunities in their local areas or those who prefer a flexible work schedule.

Remote work has also enabled companies to tap into a global talent pool and hire individuals with specialized skills, regardless of their location. This has created a level playing field for job seekers and provided them with more options in terms of finding employment.

2. New Job Roles

The rise of technology has also given birth to new job roles that were unheard of a few years ago. With the increasing use of artificial intelligence (AI), machine learning, and big data, industries such as marketing, finance, healthcare, and education have seen a surge in demand for professionals with expertise in these areas.

For instance, data scientists, AI engineers, and digital marketing specialists are some of the most in-demand job roles in today's digital age. These jobs not only offer lucrative salaries but also provide individuals with the opportunity to work on cutting-edge technology and contribute to groundbreaking innovations.

3. Increased Demand for Digital Skills

In today's digital age, having a basic understanding of technology is no longer enough. With the rapid pace at which technology is advancing, digital skills have become a prerequisite for almost every job role. From basic computer skills to proficiency in coding, digital marketing, and data analysis, these skills have become necessary for individuals to remain competitive in the job market.

Fortunately, with the wide availability of online

courses and resources, individuals can easily upskill themselves and acquire the necessary digital skills to excel in their chosen careers. This has also opened doors for individuals from various backgrounds to enter the technology industry, promoting diversity and inclusivity in the workforce.

4. Entrepreneurship Opportunities

The digital age has also paved the way for individuals to become entrepreneurs and start their own businesses. With the rise of e-commerce platforms, social media marketing, and digital advertising, starting a business has become more accessible than ever before.

The playing field has been leveled, and individuals with innovative ideas and a strong online presence can easily compete with established companies.

Moreover, the digital age has also enabled businesses to reach a wider audience and expand their customer base globally. This presents numerous opportunities for entrepreneurs to tap into new markets and grow their businesses exponentially.

5. Flexibility and Work-Life Balance

The traditional 9-5 work culture is slowly becoming a thing of the past in the digital age. With remote work and flexible schedules becoming more prevalent, individuals now have the freedom to choose when and where they work. This has allowed employees to strike a better work-life balance, leading to increased job satisfaction and productivity.

Moreover, the availability of various online tools and apps has made it easier for individuals to manage their workloads efficiently, further contributing to a healthier work-life balance.

In conclusion, the digital age has undoubtedly opened doors to countless career opportunities for individuals across various industries. With remote work, new job roles, increased demand for digital skills, entrepreneurship opportunities, and flexibility in the workplace, there has never been a better time to explore and pursue a fulfilling career. It is essential for individuals to embrace technology and continuously upskill themselves to remain competitive in the ever-evolving job market. So, take advantage of the digital age, and let it guide you towards a successful and rewarding career path.

Chapter - 10

The Future of Digitalization and Your Role in Shaping It

Technology has been advancing at a rapid pace in the last decade, and it is showing no signs of slowing down. With the rise of artificial intelligence, the Internet of Things, and other digital innovations, we are on the brink of a major digital revolution.

This digitalization is changing the way we live, work, and communicate with each other. It has also created a world of endless possibilities and opportunities for individuals and businesses alike. But what does the future hold for digitalization? And what role do we as individuals play in shaping it?

In this chapter, we will explore the future of

digitalization and the crucial role we must play in shaping it.

The Current State of Digitalization

Digitalization refers to the use of digital technologies to transform traditional processes and systems into more efficient and advanced ones. It has already revolutionized many industries such as healthcare, education, finance, and transportation. For instance, telemedicine has made it possible for doctors to remotely diagnose and treat patients. Online learning platforms have made education accessible to people from all over the world. And mobile banking has made financial services more convenient and accessible.

Digitalization has also changed the way we communicate with each other. Social media platforms have made it easier for us to connect with friends and family, while video conferencing tools have made it possible to have face-to-face communication with people from different parts of the world. But despite all these advancements, we are only at the beginning of our digital journey. The future holds even more exciting developments that will further transform our world.

The Future of Digitalization

The future of digitalization is full of possibilities. Technology experts predict that we will see an even greater integration of technologies such as artificial intelligence, virtual reality, and blockchain in our daily lives. Here are some key trends that are expected to shape the future of digitalization:

1. **Artificial Intelligence (AI):** AI is already playing a significant role in our lives, from virtual assistants like Siri and Alexa to chatbots and smart home devices. In the future, AI is expected to become even more advanced, with the ability to learn and adapt to human behavior, making our lives more convenient and efficient.

2. **Internet of Things (IoT):** The IoT refers to the network of physical devices, vehicles, home appliances, and other items embedded with

sensors, software, and network connectivity. This network allows these devices to collect and exchange data, making our lives more connected and automated. In the future, we can expect to see a more extensive use of IoT in various industries, from healthcare to manufacturing.

3. Blockchain: Blockchain is a decentralized system that stores data in the form of blocks, providing a secure and transparent way of storing and sharing information. It has already disrupted the financial industry with the rise of cryptocurrencies like Bitcoin. In the future, we can expect to see blockchain being used in other industries like supply chain management, healthcare, and voting systems.

4. Virtual Reality (VR): VR technology has already made its way into gaming and entertainment industries. But in the future, we can expect to see its use in other areas like education, training simulations, and even therapy. VR has the potential to create immersive experiences that can transform the way we learn and perceive the world around us.

Your Role in Shaping the Future of Digitalization
With the rapid pace of digitalization, it is easy to feel overwhelmed or even left behind. But as individuals, we have an essential role to play in shaping the future of digitalization. Here's how you can make a positive impact:

1. Embrace Change: The first step towards shaping the future of digitalization is to embrace change. Be open-minded and willing to learn about new technologies and their potential impact on our lives. Instead of fearing change, try to understand it and see how it can improve our daily lives.

2. Educate Yourself: The more you know about digitalization and its potential, the better equipped you will be to shape its future. Take advantage of online resources, attend workshops and conferences, and keep yourself updated with the latest technological advancements.

3. Be an Early Adopter: As new technologies emerge, be willing to try them out and provide feedback. Your input can help shape the development of these technologies and make them more user-friendly and accessible.

4. Advocate for Ethical Use of Technology: With great power comes great responsibility. As digitalization continues to advance, it is crucial to advocate for its ethical use. This includes protecting user data and privacy, promoting diversity in technology, and addressing any potential negative impacts on society.

5. Nurture Digital Skills: As the world becomes more digitally driven, having digital skills will become increasingly important. As individuals, we can play a role in nurturing these skills in ourselves and others. This can include learning coding languages, staying updated on the latest trends, and encouraging young people to pursue careers in STEM (Science, technology, engineering, and mathematics) fields.

The future of digitalization is full of endless possibilities, and as individuals, we have a significant role to play in shaping it. By embracing change, educating ourselves, being early adopters, advocating for ethical use of technology, and nurturing digital skills, we can contribute to making the world a better place with the help of technology.

So let's embrace the future with open arms and work towards creating a better tomorrow through digitalization. The possibilities are limitless; it is up to us to shape them for the better.

By

Brahmacharimayum Devdutta Sharma
Father of Digital Civilization

Brahmacharimayum Devdutta Sharma, Father of Digital Civilization

In today's era, it is impossible to imagine our lives without digitalization. From our daily activities to business operations, everything has become digitalized. And behind this digital revolution, there are pioneers who have played crucial roles in laying the foundation of the digital world we live in today. One such pioneer is Brahmacharimayum Devdutta Sharma, also known as the Father of Digital Civilization.

Sharma's contributions to the digital world are immense and cannot be ignored. His book, "Words to Teenagers," sheds light on the impact of digitalization on the younger generation, and how they can effectively navigate this ever-evolving digital world.

In his book, Sharma emphasizes the importance of understanding the digital world and its influence on our lives. He believes that in order to fully embrace and utilize the benefits of digitalization, one must first understand its potential and implications. This is especially important for teenagers, who are at a stage in their lives where they are most susceptible to the influence of technology.

One of the key topics Sharma addresses in his book is the addictive nature of digital devices and social media. With the rise of smartphones and social media platforms, teenagers have become more reliant on these tools for entertainment, communication, and validation. Sharma warns against the dangers of becoming too attached to these devices and urges teenagers to practice moderation in their usage.

He also highlights the impact of social media on body image and self-esteem among teenagers.

With the constant pressure to portray a perfect life on social media, many young people often feel inadequate and develop insecurities about their appearance and achievements. Sharma's advice to teenagers is to not compare themselves to others on social media and focus on their own growth and well-being.

Another important aspect of digitalization that Sharma addresses in his book is cyberbullying. With the rise of online platforms, bullying has taken on a whole new form and has become more prevalent among teenagers. Sharma emphasizes the importance of being aware of cyberbullying and taking necessary steps to protect oneself from it. He also urges teenagers to be responsible digital citizens and not partake in any form of online harassment.

Apart from the negative impacts, Sharma also highlights the numerous benefits of digitalization. He talks about how the internet has made knowledge and information easily accessible to everyone, breaking down traditional barriers to learning. This has opened up endless opportunities for teenagers to learn and grow in various fields.

Sharma also stresses the importance of using digital platforms for social impact and change. He encourages teenagers to use their voices and the power of social media to raise awareness about important issues and bring about positive change in society.

As the Father of Digital Civilization, Sharma also discusses the future of digitalization and its potential to further shape our lives. With advancements in technology like artificial intelligence, virtual reality, and the internet of things, he envisions a world where digitalization will continue to play a crucial role in our daily lives.

Sharma's book is a reminder that with great power comes great responsibility. As we continue to embrace digitalization and all its benefits, it is important for us, especially teenagers, to use it wisely and ethically. We must not forget the human aspect of our interactions and not let technology completely take over our lives.

In conclusion, Brahmacharimayum Devdutta Sharma's book, "Words to Teenagers," is a must-read for both teenagers and adults alike. It sheds light on the impact of digitalization on our lives and provides valuable insights on how we can navigate this new world responsibly. Sharma's contributions as the Father of Digital Civilization will continue to shape our present and future, and his words will serve as a guiding light for generations to come.